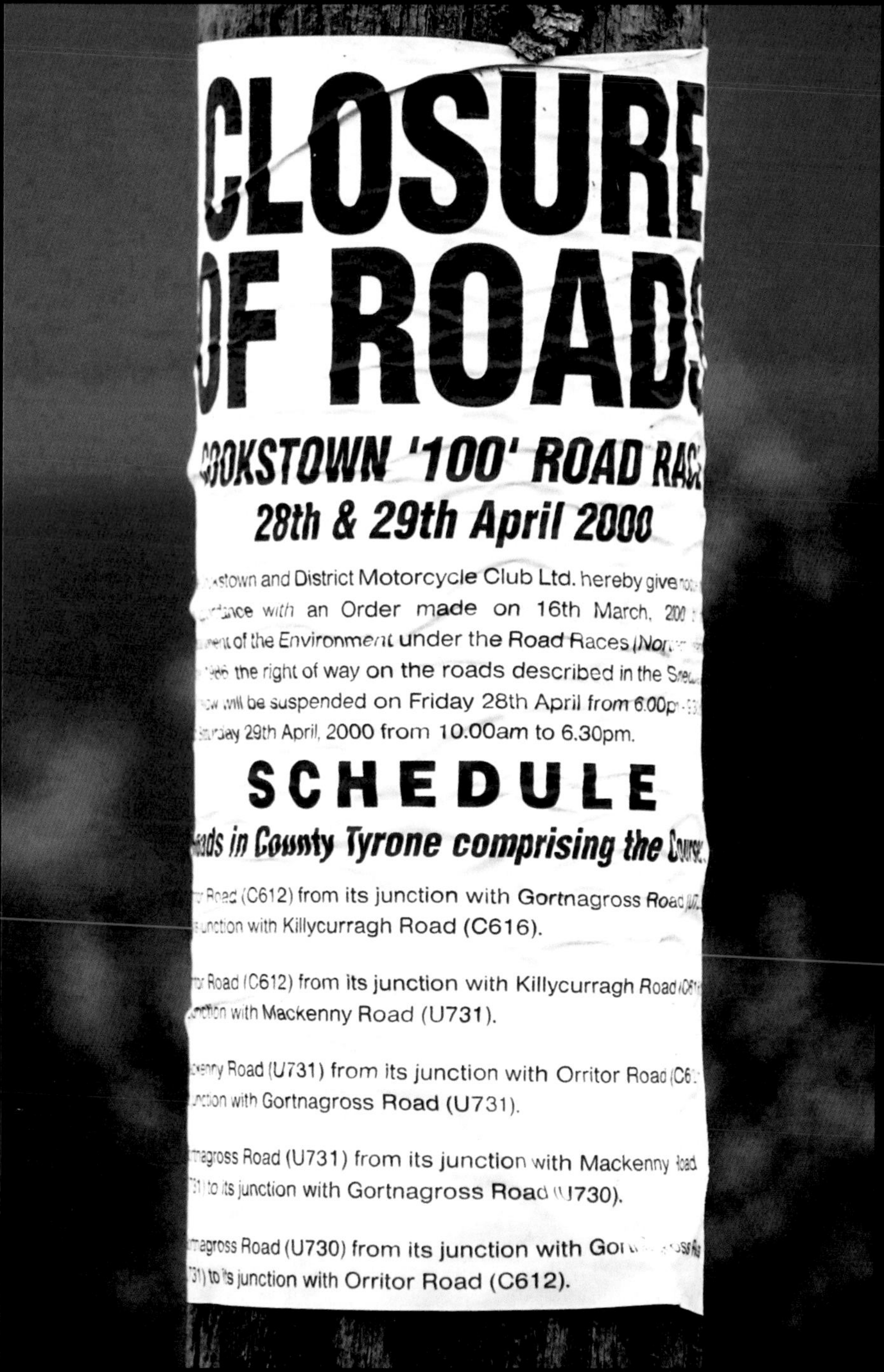

To Hazel,
Emma and Laura

Ragged EDGE

A raw and intimate portrait of road racing

STEPHEN DAVISON

BLACKSTAFF
PRESS

BELFAST

Richard Britton blasts his 600cc DMRR
Honda over the Deer's Leap at
Monaghan road races in 2004.

I sunk my fingernails into the soft leather of the Porsche seat and held on as hard as I could, watching the needle swing up the white dial: 140 – 150 – 155, until it eventually peaked at 162mph. John McGuinness, Isle of Man TT legend and the driver on this white-knuckle blast along a road where we definitely shouldn't have been doing 162mph, hit the brakes hard and looked over, 'Did that feel fast?'

'Bloody right it felt fast,' I mumbled with relief as the car slowed.

'When I rode the Monstermob Ducati at the TT in 2003 we had telemetry on the bike and it gave a reading of 184mph at the bottom of Bray Hill,' was the nonchalant response to my shaken state.

The eight-times TT winner had brilliantly and bluntly brought to a close a discussion we had been having since the evening before over a pint or two. Road racers are always asked the question 'Are you guys mad?' There is an implicit assumption that only some form of insanity could compel them to do the things they do on closed public roads on a motorcycle. Although John had actually raised the issue himself, his annoyance at the very idea of it was obvious and his response came not in words but in the way he knew best: sheer speed.

We had just hit an outlandish velocity within the protection of a four-wheeled capsule, on a wide, straight, flat and very well surfaced road. At the Isle of Man TT in 2003 John had been on two wheels and naked to the elements as he hurtled down the most fearsome drop in bike racing, on an ordinary town road, in the midst of houses, with stone walls and telegraph poles, manhole covers and kerbs for close company. And he had been going 22mph faster.

John McGuinness cranks the Monstermob Ducati through the Brandywell at the Isle of Man TT in 2003.

If you or I tried to do that we would be killed. Instantly. If a madman tried to do that he would die too. Only someone with experience and consummate skill in handling a motorcycle that actually takes off and flies over the bumps at the top of Bray Hill before beginning its terrifying descent can survive. Only someone in complete control, with lightning-quick reflexes to exert just enough force on the handlebars to skim the front wheel off the kerb on the left and then the right at 180mph-plus, can live to tell the tale. The only people who can do this are road racers, men like John McGuinness, who have built themselves up to such feats, who know exactly where those manholes are and where to avoid the bumps that would fire them straight into a solid wall.

When all of this is mastered, when the spectacular action is brought to a perfect pitch as bend flows into bend and the rises are crested right up onto the top step of the podium, there is unparalleled joy. The celebrations are louder, longer and more arduous than any race – nobody parties like road racers.

That, though, is only one side of the story. With speed like this in these places there are devastating risks. Things do go wrong, whether as a result of changing road conditions, machine failure or simply rider error. If the worst happens the outcome is in the lap of the gods; there are no good places to fall off in a road race. The financial rewards for the successful, in what is still a largely amateur sport, are few and far between. Whilst some are paid in millions for the challenge of batting a ball back and forth across a net or for chasing a little white sphere around acres of greenery, road racers still earn a pittance for risking all in their chosen sport. But that is their choice. The pull of the elemental battle of man and machine against the road in a test of speed and bravery is as old as the engine itself, but to compete against these odds has a cost and many have paid a very high price. Sometimes it is a physical cost, paid in money or in pain. Sometimes it is an emotional cost – and at times, right out on the ragged edge, it becomes a matter of life and death. In thirty years of watching and photographing road racers one thing remains constant for me; a sense of wonder as to how they do it, how they can take themselves to limits the rest of us can never even imagine. But I have also seen what it costs and I have felt it myself. That the men and women of the sport have let my lens into their story is a tribute to their openness and realism. I hope they feel that I have told it the way it is.

STEPHEN DAVISON
MAY 2005

Guy Martin gets it all in the grass on his 1000cc Suzuki at the Scarborough Esses during the Gold Cup meeting in 2004.

The Messiah
Martin Finnegan

Not since the glory days of Dubliner Eddie Laycock in
the late 1980s and early 1990s has the Republic of Ireland
had a road racer to challenge the legends from the North
– Robert and Joey Dunlop, Brian Reid, Sam McClements
and Phillip McCallen. But all that has changed in the past
couple of seasons with the rise of the 'Flying Finn'. Born
and reared within earshot of the infamous Skerries course
in County Dublin, Martin Finnegan has proven himself able
for the best the North can offer, and the crowds have
poured onto the roads to cheer their local hero in his
battles with Adrian Archibald, Richard Britton and
Ryan Farquhar. Their 'Messiah' has come.
Finnegan served his time as a schoolboy motocrosser,
starting at the tender age of nine, before being drawn
between the Irish hedges. The combination of this dirt bike
legacy, his strong build and superb fitness has created an
all-action style that has captured the imagination of race
fans. No one in road racing has ever jumped higher or
further, and smoking the tyres as he backs his 180bhp
superbike into narrow road-ends has become a Finnegan
trademark that blows many a commentator's fuse.
It isn't all show with the big man from Lusk, though.
Martin Finnegan is deadly serious about his business and is
totally focussed on the goal – winning a TT race. 'It is the
ultimate challenge and I want to conquer the Isle of Man,'
he explains. Working towards this end he has adopted
the same approach as most modern road racers in
acquiring a personal trainer, following a strict fitness
programme and eating a controlled diet. Long gone
are the days of a road racer turning up at a meeting
feeling a bit worse for wear, stubbing out a fag and
throwing his leg over the bike to race.

Martin Finnegan prepares to race at the Macau Grand Prix in 2004.

This dedication has paid dividends. After winning the Irish road race Support championship – the beginners class – in 1999 Martin moved on to become Irish Open champion in 2004. The Isle of Man bug bit hard in 2000 when he won the Manx Grand Prix Newcomers Lightweight challenge with a race and lap record that will never be broken, as the 250cc class has since disappeared from the listings. He took a huge step closer to his ultimate ambition when he stood on the TT podium for the first time in 2005, finishing third in the Superbike race. In the Senior race he established himself as the fastest Irish rider ever around the Mountain course.

Despite his success, Martin hasn't lost his down-to-earth attitude, and his local roots still provide the inspiration for his racing. As is so often the way, it was a local man who gave him the original impetus. 'Tony Carton raced himself and I used to wash his vans every week to get money to buy tyres for my motocrosser. Then he lent me one of his bikes to race on tarmac and that was it,' Martin remembers. Carton remains a sponsor as well as Finnegan's employer in the day job as a plant fitter: throughout the winter months Martin services diggers and bulldozers, and his understanding employer allows a sabbatical during the summer weeks of racing. Critically, the wage is paid all year round, easing the pressure on Finnegan's personal funds. Men like Carton, the unsung heroes of road racing, provide the money and support that every rider needs to break through into the big time. What makes their commitment all the more remarkable, and extremely rare in modern sport, is the lack of return – other than pure pleasure – on their investment.

Performing in front of an appreciative home audience on the R1 Yamaha at Duke's Bends during the Skerries 100 in 2004. Martin Finnegan has dominated his home meeting over the last four seasons, winning a treble in 2005.

Living only a stone's throw from the house he was born in, Martin drives the narrow, bumpy roads of his home course on his daily business. En route he can note every change in the Skerries road surface, every abuse that the normal traffic causes. It is that local knowledge that allows him to fire his machine through the right/left flick of Duke's Bends flat out, wrestling with the bars as the front wheel rises over the crown of the road, kicking up the dust as he brushes the bank on the exit. In the last four years Finnegan has been triumphant on the Skerries circuit, scoring a treble in 2005 against the best that Ireland – North or South – can offer. 'Nothing beats winning in front of your home crowd,' he enthuses. For fans there's nothing like watching the hometown boy do the business on the local roads.

Hail the new hero.

ABOVE: Working on a race bike in the shed at his parent's house at Lusk, County Dublin, in 2004.

LEFT: Sharing a meal at the family table in Lusk with his father Jim, mother Margaret, and brother Sean.

FAR LEFT: Martin working on the day job in a cold, muddy field at Balbriggan, County Dublin, in 2004.

Big air! Martin takes a huge leap over the biggest jump in Irish road racing on the R1 Yamaha at Dundalk in 2004, ahead of Ryan Farquhar. No one is more spectacular on the roads than Finnegan, a legacy of his schoolboy motocross days.

Ever the showman, Martin wheelies his Vitrans Honda Fireblade in the company of a military Lynx helicopter during a speed testing session at Ballykelly airfield before the North West 200 in 2005.

Martin Finnegan takes the suspension of his Vitrans
Honda Fireblade to the limit and beyond at the bottom of
Barregarrow during practice for the 2005 TT.

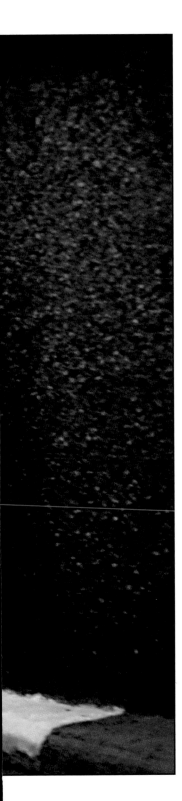

A milestone in the Finnegan career. Martin enjoys his first ever TT podium after the 2005 Superbike race in the company of John McGuinness (centre) and Adrian Archibald (left), who finished first and second.

A good day out
Irish road racing

My first day out at a motorbike race was on a sunny June morning in 1974. A couple of cousins and myself had rattled our way up to Dundrod in a rusty Ford for the Killinchy 150 meeting with our Uncle Sandy. (How many of us have been introduced to the rituals of road racing in this way?) The other boys had been to the races before and seemed more intent on picking berries and squashing them into each other's faces, but I was spellbound as soon as I heard the faint scream of the engines leaving the grid on the other side of the hill. The endless drone traced the bikes' progress down the 'Flying Kilo', briefly silenced as the throttles shut for Leathemstown corner, then growing to a remorseless roar down the awesome Deer's Leap. 'Here they come,' my uncle shouted, and the racers burst into view under the trees at Cochranstown, flying towards us in a crazy, weaving pack. I'd grown more and more scared as the noise came closer, and by the time I actually saw the bikes I was completely terrified! Standing in the hawthorn hedge, legs shaking and trying to hide my fear from the bigger boys, I was certain that the manic racers were going to come flying up the ditch and run us over. It was all too quick to take in, too fast to focus on, never mind pick out who was who – I couldn't believe how my uncle was able to mark down the first five numbers in his race programme.

Cheered on by the fans on the ditch, Richard Britton celebrates a race victory in the 600cc event at Dundalk in 2003. Richard lost his life in a crash at the final meeting of the season at Ballybunion, County Kerry, in September 2005. Very much the 'People's Champion', Richard was laid back and easy going in his approach to racing and to life and no one enjoyed a day out at a race more than he did.

Cold winter light reflects on the window of Darran Lindsay's workshop as he prepares his 250cc Honda at his Dundrod home in 2005. Darran lives on the famous race course, just a few yards from the final bend.

The winner's champagne shares space with boxes of new fairings in Ian Lougher's kitchen as he and fellow racer Stephen Thompson haggle over a deal. Road racers often supplement their racing income with sidelines such as supplying race parts or buying and selling the odd car.

One of only a few road racers who ride full-time, Ian Lougher works on the brakes of his 125cc Honda at his garage in Dromore, County Down. A Welshman by birth, Ian has now set up home in Northern Ireland.

Of course, the terror only lasted a second or two as they all flew safely past, and I had four or five minutes to take a few deep breaths and get myself together again for the second lap. Every lap I became a little more used to the speed, a little more settled into the rhythm of the day, and that day has led into countless other days spent watching motorbikes race on country lanes all over Ireland.

Back then we only went to a few races, the 'big ones' like the North West and the Ulster Grand Prix and a couple of smaller ones like the Mid-Antrim and maybe the Cookstown at the start of the season. Much has changed in Irish road racing

Always nervous before a race, Martin Finnegan dashes from the start line at Killalane in 2004 to water the cabbages.

since the 1970s, and many will lament the demise of events like the Carrowdore 100, the Killinchy 150 and the famous Temple 100, the oldest road race in the world. Safety issues and pressure from local residents and businesses brought the road closing orders for these races to an end. But they have been replaced by a plethora of new venues, mostly south of the border. Places like Athea and Dundalk, Kells and Faugheen, Glaslough and Walderstown are now established as part of a thriving Irish road racing calendar. Shops and hotels benefit from custom that would never

A tap tied to a post forms the 'shower block' in the Athea paddock in 2004.

Most road race paddocks are fields donated for the day by sympathetic farmers. At Athea in 2004 Victor Gilmore had to share parking space with the owner's tractor and slurry spreader.

usually stop at these out of the way places, and a pub or two in every village keeps the visitors happy. Whereas practice and racing used to all take place on a single day, the meetings are now run over a whole weekend in the South and on Friday evening and Saturday in the North, where there is no Sunday racing. Whilst religious and cultural differences on either side of the border have influenced the way racing is organised in the two jurisdictions, they are ignored in the paddock where the camaraderie and good humour of the racers and fans has been unaffected by issues that blight many other sports in Ireland.

It is the relaxed and easygoing nature of Irish road racing that makes it so enjoyable. The sport is still organised by unpaid volunteers, whether it be the major international events like the North West and Ulster Grand Prix or the smaller national meetings at Tandragee or Killalane.

Focussed on the road ahead, Michael Rutter gets ready to race at the 2005 North West 200.

RIGHT: Although the setting for the preparations may be primitive, when the flag drops the racing is totally committed. Ryan Farquhar, on the Harker ZX10 Kawasaki, leads the pack down to the 'Flying Kilo' at the 2004 Ulster Grand Prix.

Cranked over and without a patch of rubber on the tarmac, Martin Finnegan passes Raymond Porter at Fenton's during the 600cc race at the Mid-Antrim 150 in 2004.

Marshals and medics and a host of other helpers and handymen turn up in all weathers to run events that take many hours to organise throughout the winter months. Whilst admission is still free at most events, almost all of the riders race out of their own wallets, making road racing one of very few sports in the world where the participants pay to entertain the spectators. At times the amateur nature of the organisation can run into conflict with the growing professionalism of other aspects of the sport, but even the bigger teams are forced to rub along with the general craic, their hi-tech set-ups and hospitality units jostling with tractors and burger vans in the crowded paddocks.

Ultimately, in a sport with few financial benefits for even its most successful protagonists, everything is still held together by an underlying love of the sport, something of an anachronism in the twenty-first century.

The one thing I remember clearly from my first road race is that Neil Tuxworth was the winner. He was a hard-up racing journeyman like all the rest of the riders in the field that day, but today he is the chief of Honda Racing in Britain. Very few people ever leave road racing.

Ryan Farquhar and Ian Lougher brush elbows as they do battle on their 250cc Hondas at Kells in 2004. Once the norm but now a rarity in other forms of motorcycle sport, road racers still ride two-strokes, four-strokes, small capacity 125s and superbikes all in the one day.

You don't even have to leave your front door to watch the racing at Walderstown! Local residents have a grandstand view of Ken Doherty in action on the Donnan Suzuki in 2004.

Fans go back to the same ditches year after year to watch the latest speed merchants. Racers turn to spannering when they hang up their leathers and return to the paddock to help the next generation. Some of us even swap the pleasure of waving our programmes from the hedgerows for capturing the action on camera. When the bug bites, it bites hard and there is rarely an escape.

Over three decades the pain and pleasures of road racing have become intertwined with the pattern of my own life. I have shared the thrill and excitement of great days with my father and my uncle, and though they are no longer here, my daughters are now keen to see for themselves this sport that seems to possess their father. Life moves on and time takes its toll but in one sense nothing has changed. When I go to a road race I am still completely in awe of the speed I witness, and it is the proximity to that speed that impresses most of all. When I can sit a few feet away from a superbike flying past at over 100mph, with Martin Finnegan sawing at the bars and peering into my lens I know I am alive. Very, very alive.

A line of 1000cc superbikes steer their way down the telegraph pole-lined tunnel at Killalane road races in 2004. The straw bales and providence offer the only protection in the event of a crash.

LEFT: Every few years road racing produces a new sensation, and Lincolnshire's twenty-three-year-old Guy Martin is the latest. He was forced to race in Ireland after losing his British racing licence for slamming a laptop computer shut on the fingers of a race official during a dispute at Rockingham circuit! Guy immediately made his mark, winning the 2003 Irish Support championship. In 2004 he lapped the TT at 122mph as a newcomer and established himself as a front runner amongst the senior opposition on the Irish roads. At times his youthful exuberance has got the better of him, as in this spectacular highside during the 250cc race in front of Ryan Farquhar at Dundalk in 2004. Fortunately, Guy was unhurt.

Guy Martin shaves in his summer home, a converted truck that he parks up in his sponsor's yard between race meetings.

Evening sunlight highlights the concentration on Bruce Anstey's face as he fights the 600cc TAS Suzuki over Black's Jump in practice for the 2005 Cookstown 100.

Riding the 1000cc O'Kane Suzuki like a horse,
Richard Britton rises out of the saddle to steady
it over the Kells jumps in 2003.

The slogan on the ice-cream van says 'Summer's Here', but a week of heavy rain turned the paddock at the 2005 Tandragee 100 road races into a quagmire and left the riders steering their machines through the liquid mud to the grid.

Race fans at the Cookstown 100 in 2004 have a grandstand view of a battle between Richard Britton and Adrian Archibald in the opening Superbike race.

Irish road racing competition has never been closer than in the last few seasons. Four, five and six men on a variety of machines regularly battle for victory at unbelievable speed. Nor has the sport ever been more popular, with huge crowds flocking to races all over the country.

Ian Lougher leads the high-speed train of Bruce Anstey, Richard Britton, Ryan Farquhar and Adrian Archibald through Dawson's Bend in the 600cc Supersport race at the 2004 Ulster Grand Prix. This was arguably the finest Irish road race of all time, with the lead and the lap record constantly changing hands throughout before Bruce Anstey snatched the win with a daring move on the final bend.

ABOVE: The 600cc class has produced the closest battles in Irish road racing over the last decade. The class was boosted by the creation of the lucrative Regal series, the brainchild of Ireland's 'Mr Road Racing', David Wood, which aimed at matching the bikes evenly by keeping them as close as possible to a standard specification. The races have regularly produced brilliant multi-rider and manufacturer tussles. In one such battle, the Production race at the 2003 Ulster Grand Prix, Richard Britton and Ryan Farquhar try to keep their Kawasakis in touch with Adrian Archibald's Suzuki and Darran Lindsay's Yamaha as Honda-mounted Ian Lougher heads the pack at Tournagrough bends.

LEFT: The 2004 600cc Production race at the Ulster Grand Prix generated a fantastic dogfight as Bruce Anstey's TAS Suzuki headed John McGuinness's IFS Yamaha and Ryan Farquhar's McAdoo Kawasaki into the bottom of Tournagrough.

37

A packed grid led by Michael Rutter (No. 2), Steve Plater (No. 9) and John McGuinness (No. 21) blasts off for the start of the opening Superbike race at the 2005 North West 200 at Portrush. Attracting the finest entry of any road race in the world and a crowd of almost 100,000, the North West 200 has become Ireland's largest sporting event.

The undisputed modern master of the North West 200 course, Michael Rutter wheelies the HM Plant Honda Fireblade over Black Hill during the 2005 event. Eleven times a North West winner, Rutter broke the 200mph top speed barrier for the first time ever on a British Isles race course at the 2004 North West 200.

Bruce Anstey cranks the 1000cc TAS Suzuki through Budore bend at 170mph during the 2003 Ulster Grand Prix. In 2004, Anstey established the Dundrod circuit as the fastest motorcycle race course in the world when he lapped it at 129.038mph, a fitting position for the course that once hosted a round of the Grand Prix world championship.

To the joy of the spectators in the Faugheen hedgerows, Darran Lindsay celebrates on the slowing-down lap of the 2004 Grand Final. Always a crowd pleaser, Lindsay continued his display in spite of the fact that he had been disqualified after falling off and remounting in the race!

Although a scruffy farm trailer acts as a rudimentary podium for the Athea road race presentations in 2005, some attention was given to decorum with the trophy table's fine white tablecloth.

Where every Irish road race eventually ends up – in the pub.
Fans enjoy a post-race pint at Athea in 2004.

DJ–JD

David Jefferies
Joey Dunlop

This pair may have had a great deal in common – both road racing legends, both masters of the TT, both record-breaking superstars – but they were never going to be soul mates. Big, brash, bold David Jefferies versus small, shy, silent Joey Dunlop. Sparks flew between them in their clashes on and off the track. With DJ it was all action and aggression: if the bike didn't want to go there, he lifted it and put it there, even if it was doing 150mph at the time. Smooth and flowing was more the JD way: precise on his racing line, exciting but not excitable. Each of them was larger than life in his own inimitable way. In the paddock no one was more photogenic than the unaffected Dunlop, whether he was quietly tinkering with some minor detail or performing a complete engine strip-down in full public view. Jefferies, constantly aware of the camera and the power of good PR, was always ready to perform a huge burnout or pull a face for the lens.

Scenes from another era. David Jefferies enjoys a pint in the TT Press room after victory in the 2002 Formula One race. Sadly, this longstanding ritual, with the first three riders visiting the Press room after the podium to chat with reporters over a leisurely drink, has disappeared with the removal of the bar following modernisation of the facility.

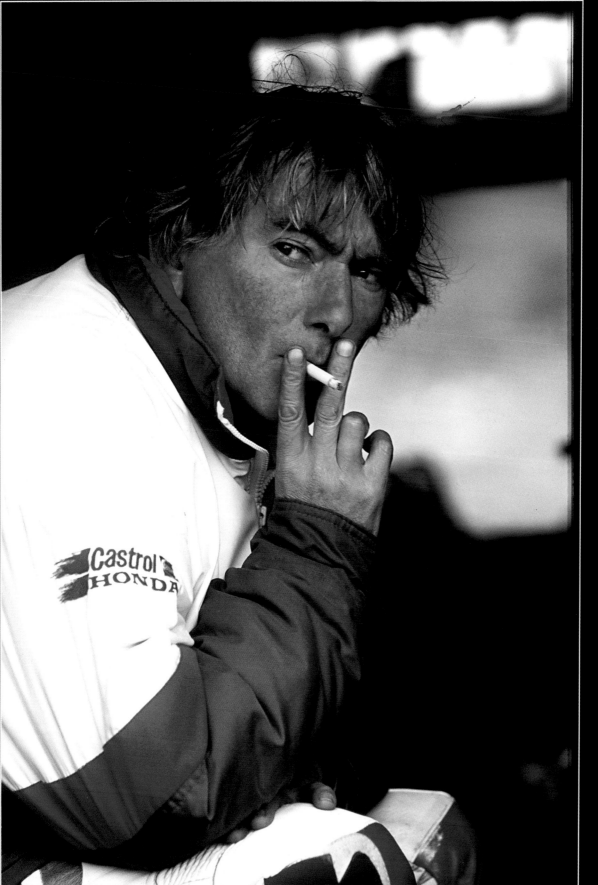

A smoker for most of his life, Joey Dunlop takes a puff in the back of his van at Dundrod in 1994. In his later years he gave up cigarettes and became ardently anti-smoking.

The Yorkshireman burst onto the road race scene with three wins at the 1999 North West 200 on V&M Yamahas. Relatively unknown up to that point, Jefferies went on to hammer home his new-found dominance with another treble at that year's Isle of Man TT, beating the ageing Dunlop in the Formula One race and robbing Honda of their unbroken record in that race since 1981. In the following two TTs he went on to score a famous treble of trebles. No respecter of reputations, for him everyone was there to be beaten and DJ had the power and the self-belief to do it. In 1999, it seemed natural that the grey-haired Dunlop, then forty-seven years old, would give way to the new colossus of road racing.

The diminutive Ulsterman looked physically weak alongside the immensely strong Englishman, and his devastation at defeat in that Formula One TT was painfully obvious. Afterwards, in the winners' enclosure, he stared straight through my camera as he searched in vain for consolation.

FAR LEFT: Evening sunlight filtering into his helmet, Joey crests Quarry Hill on the RC45 Honda during North West 200 practice in 1999. The following winter Honda presented this machine to Joey as a gift to mark his twentieth year of association with the Japanese factory and it became a feature in his Ballymoney bar, where he suspended it from the ceiling. But with no superbike to race when Honda failed to supply a machine after the 2000 TT, Joey took the RC45 down again for his final trip to Estonia where he won on it for the last time.

LEFT: En route to his final treble of treble TT wins in 2002, DJ cranks through Creg Ny Baa with Kate's Cottage shining in the sun in the background.

47

ABOVE: I never saw Joey Dunlop more relaxed and happy than at the Isle of Man TT in 2000, where he appeared to be enjoying the adulation that came from winning three races. He had hankered after another big bike win, and that famous Formula One victory produced an inner contentment that we all could share in.

LEFT: 'This is my new toy!' Ask any of David Jefferies' friends what he was like and they will often describe him as a 'big kid'. During this photoshoot at the TAS Suzuki headquarters, at the start of what was to be his final season, DJ was in great form, making jokes and clowning around for the camera. His team's racing heritage can be glimpsed behind the white backdrop, where the famous Hector Neill RG 500 Suzuki, a bike raced by Joey Dunlop amongst many others, stands in pristine condition.

A year later it was a very different story as Joey scored perhaps his most famous TT win, storming to victory on the SP1 Honda in the 2000 Formula One event (this was to be the last win ever in that race for the once dominant Honda factory). The previous August, JD had exorcised some of the DJ demons with a brilliant win against the burly Yorkshireman at the Ulster Grand Prix, but this Formula One victory was on a different scale. With 24 TT wins already under his belt to guarantee his status as a legend, Joey added two more to underpin his supremacy on the Isle of Man.

Jefferies fired a strong salvo back towards the Ulsterman, taking three TT wins himself in 2000, including victory in the Senior TT at the end of the week, and smashing the 125mph lap barrier for the first time on the Mountain course. Road racing had its latest clash of the titans, with the relative newcomer Jefferies matching every move the seemingly everlasting Dunlop made.

Of course, we had been here before with Joey Dunlop. That is what made him so very, very special in the sport. Over the past twenty-odd years there had been lots of princes to Dunlop's king of the roads. Usually they were younger, more aggressive and more outspoken than the introverted Ballymoney man.

But whether it was McCallen or Jefferies, or even his own brother, Robert, Joey had at some point

The moments before the start of a race are always a special time for photographs. The new fad of television cameras sticking their lenses into the riders' helmets and recording 'Hello Mum' messages from extremely self-conscious and ill-at-ease racers is a miserable substitute for images of the quiet moments of reflection and intense concentration like these of Jefferies at the 2003 North West 200 (right) and Dunlop (far right) at the 1995 Ulster Grand Prix. Although DJ would pull the odd face for the camera if he was in the mood, when it was finally down to business everything else was closed out. As for Joey Dunlop – well, let's just say I never saw him give a 'thumbs up' in his life.

exposed their flaws, shown they were beatable when they had appeared invincible, and proved that he was still a force to be reckoned with. He had seen them all come and go and he was still there, still at the top. No other motorcycle racer has ever given so many people so much pleasure over such a long period of time.

Then, in July 2000, on a wet and dreary Sunday afternoon on a winding road through an Estonian pine forest, it all came to a sudden end. When I visited the shady spot where Joey Dunlop lost his life on the first anniversary of his death, what struck me most was how, after all those races he'd ridden in, all those podiums he'd stood on over the thirty-one years of his racing career, it had all ended so quickly. In a split second a back wheel had spun sideways, followed immediately by the crunching of plastic sliding on the wet tarmac, the dull thud of silver leathers against a tree, and that glorious life was over.

Almost unbelievably DJ met a similar fate three years later in what is probably the fastest-ever road racing crash. Flat out in top gear entering Crosby village in practice at the 2003 TT, his TAS Suzuki's rear wheel skidded out from below him and he was killed instantly, hurled into a stone wall at almost 180mph. Within a couple of seasons, road racing was robbed of its two best riders. The very nature of their deaths remains shrouded in mystery. Was there, as has been claimed, a line of spilled oil on the road as DJ blasted into Crosby that sunny Thursday afternoon? If so, why did his team-mate Adrian Archibald, who was just yards in front of him, not crash too? Jefferies had not seemed his usual happy-go-lucky self in 2003. He appeared under pressure, battling with his weight as he struggled with the Suzukis and a more confident team-mate. Usually relaxed and playful in front of the camera, he was guarded and prickly at the TT, and on the morning of that final Thursday practice I had never seen him so intense as he sat on the bike in the paddock, making it patently clear he did not want to be photographed.

Dunlop's demise was similarly enigmatic. Distraught following the suicide of an old friend and sponsor, he had set off on the long trek to Estonia alone. Those who met him in Tallin say he was relaxed, but there is no doubt he had left home a troubled man. We will never know for sure what caused the crash or Joey's death. I spoke to the young rider who followed Joey into that final bend and he said that Joey's machine had been sliding badly on the wet roads in previous corners. As with DJ, we are left wondering what really happened. Why was it that something they had done thousands and thousands of times before suddenly went so badly wrong in those single moments? Perhaps it is fitting for legends to depart in this way. Just as we were never really able to figure out how they could go so incredibly fast on a racing motorcycle, it is equally elusive why it all came to such a sudden end.

JD and DJ share the podium after the final Superbike race at the 1999 Ulster Grand Prix. It had been an incredible day for both men. Jefferies, suffering from an injured left wrist (hence the glove), had won on his debut at Dundrod and set a new outright lap record for the course. Joey had ridden one of the races of his life on Irish soil to beat the seemingly invincible Yorkshireman. Dunlop's final lap, the last he was to ride at his favourite circuit, was his fastest ever around Dundrod.

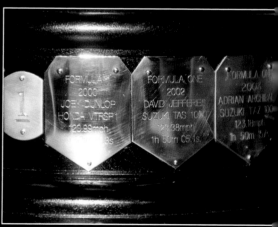

The two legends' names are engraved side by side on the winners' plaques decorating the Formula One TT trophy.

Ryan's Road

Ryan Farquhar

In 2004 Ryan Farquhar got married, became a professional road racer, suffered a career-threatening injury, had a major operation, won thirty races including his first TT, signed a contract to race 'works' Kawasakis and became a father. For most of that extraordinary year I was beside him with my camera, documenting the highs and lows. To get good photographs a photographer needs good access, and to gain that access there must be trust. Somehow or other the two of us always worked it out, and Ryan was incredibly generous with his time. But knowing someone this well can have its drawbacks when it comes to making pictures. There might not be enough distance, the subject can play to the camera, or the photographer can be inhibited by not wanting to show an unflattering side. Again, we always seemed to work it out. Ryan never hid and I never turned my back. Now hitting his thirtieth year, Ryan has become the hottest property on the road racing scene. Another TT win in 2005, and a record that has seen him win on every road circuit he has raced in Britain and Ireland has secured him that position. But it's not one that has come easily for the man who hails from the tiny hamlet of Killyman in County Tyrone. His first year as a pro ended on the operating table, with surgeons chiselling a piece of bone out of his pelvis to graft into the dead scaphoid bone in the wrist he had injured during training at the start of the season.

Ryan Farquhar takes a break from his punishing training schedule in a misty County Tyrone bog, a few miles from his Killyman home.

At work on his shed's pride and joy – the two-ton lathe. Ryan often makes special components for his race bikes himself.

RIGHT: The wooden shed at the side of Ryan's semi in the hamlet of Killyman is where he can be found on most winter evenings, building his race bikes. The shed was built around a two-ton lathe that came with his engineering apprenticeship, and he used a crane to set it on the concrete floor before building the walls up around it. Farquhar follows in a tradition of self-reliance amongst road racers, and the wealth of tools and skills at his disposal means he rarely has to leave the cosy confines of his workshop to seek assistance.

Ryan had opted to race on in agony throughout the year, knowing that each ride was killing the bone a little bit more, and ended up having this make-or-break operation. Fortunately, the procedure was a success.

The decision to race on through the pain was not taken out of bloody mindedness or bravado but out of necessity: Ryan had given up his day job and had a wife to support, with their first baby on the way. Prize money offered the only income, and the first TT win eased some of the pressure. There's an old adage in bike racing that becoming a father takes half a second per lap off your speed, the thought of not seeing that tiny wee face again just taking the edge off the throttle hand. But Ryan offers a different perspective – his new commitment to family and home will, he feels, drive him to go faster as he has a greater need to win, to earn the money to support his dependants. Major wins in 2005 seem to bear out his theory. His loved ones are certainly there to support him at every race meeting, and like most road racers, Ryan looks to a familiar retinue for support.

RIGHT: **Pounding out the miles. Ryan's image is reflected in a bog pool in the Peatlands park in County Tyrone where he runs half a dozen miles every day. 'The moss isn't so hard on my knees and ankles,' he explains. Some of the top Irish road racers, like Adrian Archibald and Martin Finnegan, have personal trainers to assist them in their battle for fitness.**

A keen cyclist, Ryan does several 30-mile stints on his pushbike every week on top of his running and gym work.

The family nature of the road racing scene is much lauded, and rightly so. In a sport as dangerous as this the main man must have complete faith in those around him who work on the bike and be able to rely on trusted faces for advice and encouragement. Sometimes it's the encouragement to win that's needed, at other times it's the reassurance that it was alright to lose. Whilst Ryan is a figure who has been outspoken and involved in controversy with race authorities throughout his career, it is a telling point that he has enjoyed a good rapport with his sponsors, who have all been involved with him for lengthy periods and who know him best. Ryan's rise to prominence has been built on dedication and commitment. He follows a rigorous physical training programme, and finding the time to devote to such a strict regime was one of the principal factors behind his decision to give up the day job servicing diggers and plant equipment.

Winning on the Isle of Man is still the ultimate goal for any road racer, and in 2004 Ryan realised this ambition with his first TT win in the Production 600cc event on the McAdoo Kawasaki. It was the Japanese factory's first four-stroke TT victory, and this bike now sits in the Kawasaki museum in Japan.

LEFT: The final day of the 2004 TT race week was 'Irish Day'. Ryan shared his win with Ballymoney's Adrian Archibald, who won the Senior TT.

BELOW: The victor's spoils. Ryan enjoys the view from the top step of the TT podium in 2004.

It is a sacrifice eagerly made in the battle to succeed and it is not without its rewards; not many plant fitters are asked for their autographs.

That remark is neither facetious nor smug. It underpins what motivates many of the young men who take up racing. Motorcycle road racing is a blue-collar sport: the racers are drawn from the ranks of mechanics and builders rather than engineers and architects. The machines used are available over the counter and most of the guys have the skills to work on the bikes themselves.

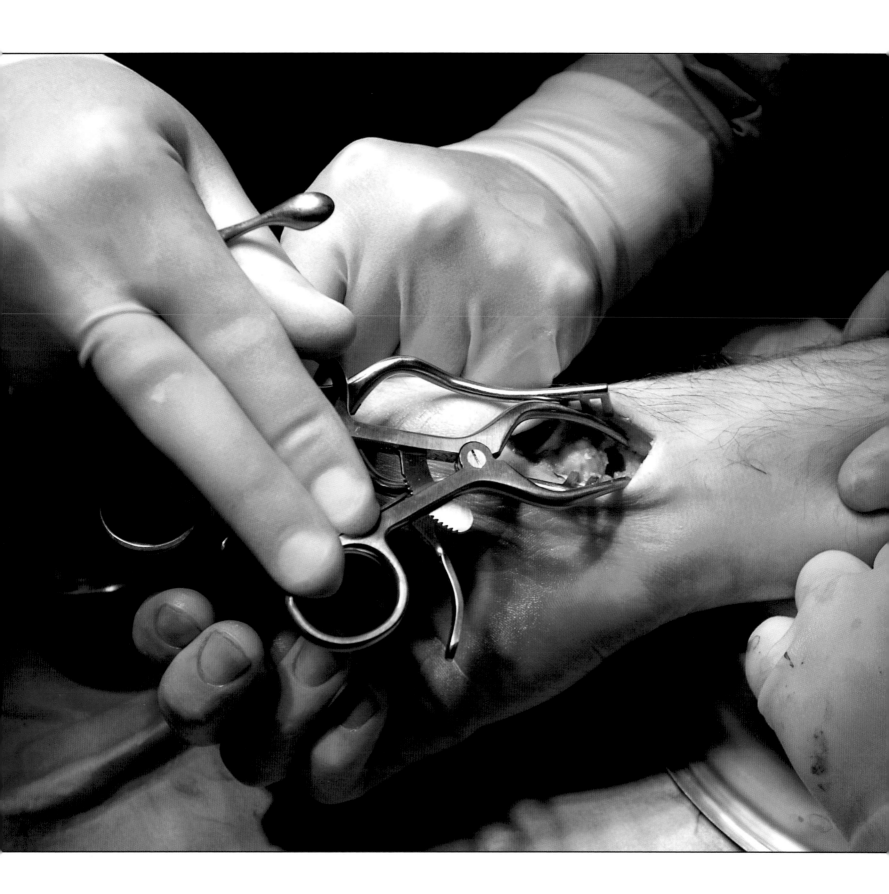

LEFT: Ryan Farquhar broke the scaphoid bone in his right wrist in a pre-season quad bike accident in 2004. Forced to race throughout the year with the injury, the bone never healed and surgeons had to perform a bone graft operation during the winter to save his racing career.

BELOW: A surgeon uses a club hammer to chisel a piece of bone from Ryan's pelvis to wire into his wrist. As he taps away with all the care of a sculptor, his colleague is preparing Ryan's wrist to insert the shaped nugget of bone needed for the successful graft. This is the pain behind the podium, the sacrifice and misery we rarely ever see. Fortunately, the delicate procedure has been a complete success.

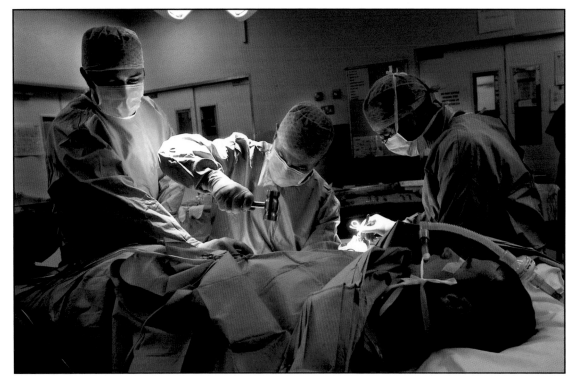

If you are good you can make money and earn some recognition; you get to spray champagne from the podium as the crowd cheers, and your picture is in the papers. We all want some recognition for what we do but that is rarely forthcoming if you're a plumber or a painter. For those with the talent and the bravery, road racing temporarily alleviates the drudgery and lets the heart soar. Of course, there is also plenty of drudgery in preparing to race. On most evenings Ryan Farquhar can be found in the wooden shed at the side of his Killyman home, fettling the bikes and engines. This has been a way of life since 1993, when he started racing. Two years later, in his first season on the roads, he had immediate success, with a podium at the Cookstown 100. As his success has grown Ryan's feet have remained firmly planted on the ground. But the sport wouldn't allow it to be any other way – no one would get away with acting like a prima donna in the road race paddock.

There are sponsors and then there are men like Kenny Harker. Affectionately known as 'the Bear' in the team, Kenny is more of a father figure to Ryan than simply the man who supplies the racing hardware. Wherever Ryan is, Kenny won't be far away.

Overcome with the emotion of the moment that they both struggled so hard to achieve, Ryan is hugged by his wife Karen after his first TT win, in 2004.

It is the complete absence of pretentious behaviour that makes it such a pleasure to work with people like Ryan. I have never yet met a road racer who had his head up his own backside. Guys like John McGuinness, Martin Finnegan and Ryan Farquhar ask you round to their house for a cup of tea or put you up for the night after a heavy session at the bar.

In 2004 I travelled to Scarborough for the Gold Cup meeting with the Farquhar team. When we arrived Ryan asked me if I knew the Oliver's Mount circuit. I told him that it had been twenty years since my last visit and that I'd forgotten most of it. 'Come on,' he said, and then walked me around the whole three-mile-long course, pointing out the best corners and spots for pictures. Can you imagine the likes of Beckham or Rooney doing something like that?

Those who matter most. Ryan Farquhar became a father for the
first time in 2004 with the birth of his baby daughter, Keeley.

Most road racers have some superstition or other, whether it is wearing a lucky pair of underpants or the way they put their boots on. For Ryan Farquhar, TT success depends upon him having a special word with the fairies at the Isle of Man's Fairy Bridge. Saying hello to the fairies at the bridge is an ancient Manx tradition purported to ensure good luck, and in racing circles it was made famous by Joey Dunlop, who always had a word for them when he arrived on the island for the TT. Ryan has taken it a stage further, visiting the bridge on the morning of each race day to seek guidance from the 'little people'. When he first told me about it, I thought he was pulling my leg, until the day I went with him to photograph his visit. I realised he was deadly serious when he nudged me and told me to say hello to them as well!

OPPOSITE: The reeds blow in the mountain wind as Ryan Farquhar skims the banks at the 32nd Milestone on the way to his second TT victory, in the 2005 Supersport event.

Ellen Vannin
Isle of Man TT

This is my Isle of Man 'office', a wonderful place to go to work with a camera on a bright June evening when the mountain road is bathed in sunlight and there isn't so much as a breath of wind. By the time the racers get to Guthrie's they have covered almost two thirds of the famous TT course, flown past places with evocative Manx names steeped in road racing history: Bradden, Greeba, Ballacraine, Creg Willy's, Cronk y Voddy, Barregarrow, Ballaugh, Kerrowmoar, Glentramman, the Gooseneck. By now they have ridden the superfast stretches between the Glencrutchery Road start line and Ballacraine before diving between the craggy walls of Glen Helen and climbing up onto the open ground that runs down into Kirk Michael village. Hammering through narrow streets lined with old-fashioned grocery shops and quaint cottages and on to Ballaugh, past the village's Raven pub and a quick blast to another hostelry at Ginger Hall, then down through the bumpy, tree-shrouded roads of Lezayre into Ramsey town before starting the steep climb up to my mountain perch. There are still the open moors to traverse, the fast-flowing curves of the Verandah and the 32nd Milestone to negotiate, before skimming down into civilisation again past Creg Ny Baa to the outskirts of Douglas and the finish line.

The water of Ramsey Bay sparkles in the evening sunlight as Nigel Connole and Denis Lowther climb up to Guthrie's Memorial bends in their 600cc Honda outfit during practice for the 2004 TT.

Thirty-seven-and-three-quarter miles per lap amounts to 226.5 miles in a six-lap Superbike race and two solid hours of racing, with the winner averaging over 126mph.

The Isle of Man TT is without parallel in modern motor sport. No other place can boast such an illustrious history as the Mountain circuit, but then few other races are ninety-eight years old (the TT will celebrate its centenary in 2007). Nor can any other course summon up such a glorious list of who's who in bike racing. Agostini, Duke, Fogarty, Hailwood, Ivy, McIntyre, Redman, Surtees, Taveri, Woods – there is a champion for almost every letter in the alphabet. The TT is steeped in tradition and draws you inexorably into its vault of nostalgia and legend. That is all part of its attraction – this glorious past that you can immerse your soul in. You want to go there, to stand at those places and imagine Hailwood screaming through the mountain mist on a Honda Six.

But such moments of unbridled pleasure are always tempered with exposure to an ever-present brutality. Never a year goes by without someone being killed racing there. Over two hundred men and women have perished competing in the TT and thousands more have been injured, many disabled for life.

A lot of the legends surrounding the race are built upon riders who have died in action.

Ballaugh Bridge is one of the most famous landmarks and photographic locations on the Isle of Man because of the jump over this severest of humpbacks. Approached flat out, the riders slow to a pedestrian 40mph or so to hop over the bridge that marks the entrance to the village. Almost everyone has their own style here, but few are as spectacular as John McGuinness was on the R1 Yamaha in 2004.

The journalist who took me on my first-ever lap of the course seemed to spend most of the trip pointing out memorials to riders who had died in crashes at those spots. The TT can be a very cruel place.

No one can fully appreciate the dangers unless they go and see for themselves the sheer speed at which these roads are being ridden. I sat on a footpath at Glentramman in 2005 and watched Archibald, McGuinness and the rest brush the kerb almost flat out in top gear as they threaded together three blindingly quick bends, with dry stone walls and huge oak trees hemming in their incredible courage and skill. It was as if God had the riders on a string and was pulling them through the vortex at supernatural speed. Divine or not, these road racers were performing in another dimension, a place unknown to ordinary mortals.

The sheer thrill of being there, feeling the sting of their speed, is what makes us road racing people. But it is always tinged with guilt. How can we justify revelling in such excitement when it costs so much in human suffering for those who get it wrong?

This jump on the run down into Ramsey town is an altogether different affair. The bikes are literally flying, propelled into the air by outrageous speed over what appears to ordinary traffic as no more than a little rise in the road. Here Bruce Anstey on the TAS Suzuki is being chased by Jason Griffiths on the R1 Yamaha as Anstey skims his way to victory in the 2004 Production 1000cc TT. It is pictures like this that make the Isle of Man photographs so different to the increasingly anodyne images from modern Moto GP.

How can we call something in which death plays such a big part 'our sport'? What fool would claim that winning a TT is worth risking your life for?
And yet ...

Teammate Ian Lougher and close friend John McGuinness pour champagne down the back of David Jefferies' leathers after he won the 2002 Senior TT. This was to be Jefferies final TT podium.

No reference could be made to the modern TT era without mention of David Jefferies. His rise to TT stardom was meteoric, making an enormous impact in a few short but glorious years. Jefferies scored treble wins in 1999, 2000 and 2002 and he became the first man to lap the Mountain course in under eighteen minutes.

DJ in full cry on the 1000cc Production TAS Suzuki at Rhencullen in 2002.

Ask any of the men or women who want to race there – and the race is over-subscribed with entries – and they will tell you that there is nothing else like it, no other challenge or thrill to rival it. Very few entertain the thought of even covering the costs of their racing, never mind actually winning any money, but they travel from every corner of the globe to take part. Men like Robert Dunlop even come back after the place has left their bodies broken and scarred for the rest of their lives. Why?
The simple answer has to be because it is there. Just as Everest beckons mountaineers, Snaefell is a magnet for motorcycle racers.

The treacherous Mountain course is there to be conquered, its dangers met face to face and beaten down. Laudably, safety improvements are constantly being made, but it can only ever be made safer, never safe. If it were easy, the people who race the TT wouldn't be interested. For them it is all very straightforward. If you win the two big bike races you get about £50,000 in today's money and you can celebrate by buying a Porsche like John McGuinness's. If you survive and finish 38th you go back to work as a motor mechanic or house painter on Monday morning with a heightened sense of your own being and a much emptier pocket. Racing the TT is all about stepping up to the mark and finding new limits for your inner self.

If you get it wrong you go home in an ambulance or a coffin; everyone knows exactly how it works. 'It's never going to happen to me' is a big part of the coping strategy, and the angst suffered by the rest of us as we wonder how long the TT can survive or whether we are trying to justify the unjustifiable is meaningless to the racers. They have done what they wanted to do, were happy doing it, and the lucky ones are already looking forward to next year.

A delighted Lougher waves to the Grandstand crowd from the top of the podium after his 2005 victory.

In 2005 Ian Lougher celebrated twenty-one years of competition at the Isle of Man TT with a brilliant win in the first Supersport event on his 600cc Honda. It was the diminutive Welshman's seventh TT victory. Lougher made his debut on the island in the 1983 Manx Grand Prix, sharing the Newcomers podium with Steve Hislop and Robert Dunlop, two other men who went on to achieve TT greatness.

In a study of neat cornering, Ian Lougher cranks the 600cc DMRR Honda through Signpost on his way to victory in the 2005 Supersport A TT.

Joey rounds Bradden Bridge in the 1998 Ultra-Lightweight TT, watched by hundreds of spectators in the packed grandstand at Bradden church. Since Dunlop's demise the crowds attending the TT have diminished, and this grandstand in particular is now half empty on race days.

With twenty-six TT wins in twenty-five years of racing in the Isle of Man, Joey Dunlop is the most successful rider in the race's almost hundred-year history. If you ask any current rider how difficult it is to win one TT, they will tell you all about the need for good pit stops, for mechanical perfection, for accurate signalling, for plenty of good luck and much more. Joey Dunlop made all those things happen twenty-six times over. His closest rival in the all-time winners' list, Mike Hailwood, won just over half Dunlop's total. It is almost certainly a record that will never be broken.

ABOVE: This is the last photograph I ever took of Joey Dunlop. After the Senior TT it is traditional that the winner meets the scouts who man the ancient lap score board at the grandstand. Although Joey had finished third behind David Jefferies the scouts asked for him and he happily signed autographs and posed for pictures with the youngsters. In the midst of all that relaxed happiness it was impossible to imagine that within a month he would be dead.

'Slow down, roads bite back.' Adrian Archibald ignores the warning sign as he hurtles through the narrow streets of Kirk Michael village on the 1000cc TAS Suzuki during practice for the 2004 TT.

Ready for business, Adrian Archibald comes to the line
as No. 1 for the 2004 Senior TT. He won the race.

Ballymoney man Adrian Archibald, a
protégé of fellow County Antrim
townsman Joey Dunlop, made his
mark on the TT in 2003. Following the
harrowing death of their teammate
David Jefferies in practice, the TAS
Suzuki squad were going to withdraw
from the event until DJ's mother
Pauline insisted that they continue to
race. Archibald rose to the occasion,
winning both the Formula One and
Senior TTs, and repeating his Senior
success in 2004.

One of the TT's most stylish riders, Adrian Archibald skims the railings
at Glentramman during the Production 1000cc TT in 2004.

Cornering in mid-air, Martin Finnegan takes Union Mills bridge with both wheels of the Vitrans Honda Fireblade off the ground during the 2005 Superbike TT.

Undoubtedly the two current TT racers hungriest for success are Martin Finnegan and Ryan Farquhar. Hailing from either side of the Irish border, both are now riding top-class machinery and have already made a significant impact. Finnegan scored his first TT podium in 2005 with third place in the Superbike race, became the fastest Irishman in the Senior, and the third fastest racer of all time at the TT with a lap of 127.014mph. Farquhar has won two 600cc TTs, for his former sponsor Winston McAdoo in 2004, and for the MSS Discovery team in 2005. Friendly towards each other off the track, Finnegan and Farquhar are intense rivals on it and offer an exciting future for the TT.

Ryan Farquhar makes a spectacular, if slightly askew, front wheel landing at Ballaugh Bridge on the MSS Discovery ZX10 Kawasaki in 2005. Ryan almost always lands like this at Ballaugh and is amazed when he sees the pictures. 'It just feels like both wheels are touching down together,' he says.

Southern 100

The famous Mountain course isn't the only venue for road racing on the Isle of Man. The Billown circuit in the southern part of the island plays host to two events: the post-TT races (which take place the day after the TT ends) and the Southern 100 in July. Unlike the TT, where the bikes leave the line individually at ten-second intervals, these are mass-start races where the racers hurtle around a 4.25-mile track that is almost continuously lined with solid stone walls. Revelling in wonderful placenames like Ballawhetstone and Cross Four Ways, the Southern 100 meeting has been graced with many world champions during its fifty-year history. Once again, Joey Dunlop is the most successful competitor at Billown, with forty-two course wins, but other Irishmen have made their mark here too. Raymond McCullough was the first man to break the 90mph lap barrier in 1975, and Brian Reid topped the 'ton' in 1983.

Sidecar duo Dave Molyneux and Craig Hallam inspect the stone walls at Iron Gate during the Southern 100 in 2003.

Ryan Farquhar has no time to call in for a cup of tea at Ballabeg cottages as he blasts past the open doors on his 400cc Kawasaki during the 2003 Southern 100.

Sandwiched between the stone walls at Church Bends,
Darran Lindsay steers his 600cc Honda through the rain
during the wet and windy Southern 100 of 2004.

I was sitting in a drain being eaten alive by midges at Joey's Bend during an evening practice session of the TT in 2004 when I saw a little brown bird alight in the middle of the road. The road was silent but I could hear a bike approaching the corner and I silently prayed that the bird would stay put until the bike appeared. As Nigel Davies cranked his 1000cc Suzuki through the right-hander, the bird took flight and I fired off several frames. Only one frame, this one, had the bird still in it. It is a special photograph for me. You only ever get a picture like this once in a lifetime, and only if you are very, very lucky. It is like catching a lightning strike. The bird was completely unhurt and flew off singing its heart out that it had escaped a brush with death. After the picture appeared in newspapers there was a great flurry of debate as to what kind of bird it actually is.

The consensus amongst the finest ornithological minds in Ireland is that it is a meadow pipit. To me it is still a wee brown birdie that was, like myself, in exactly the right place at the right time on that charmed evening.

Pain

A frightened Phillip McCallen ponders what might have been as he displays the wreckage of his leathers after a 150mph crash at Quarry Bends in the 1997 Lightweight (250cc) TT.

A sombre 2003 Formula One TT podium pays its respects to David Jefferies who had been killed two days previously. His close friend John McGuinness pays his own tribute as he glances heavenwards.

Defeat for Joey Dunlop in the 1999 Formula One TT was almost unbearable.

One of the biggest problems in covering the Isle of Man TT is that I always have to try to get back to the Grandstand for the podium presentations after every race. With only a few access roads, loads of traffic and tight deadlines, this has led to some unofficial TTs 'off course' as I race back and forward in the hire car! But they are journeys worth the effort to capture the mixed emotions of the racing men when they pull off their helmets and the masks slip away to reveal their pain and joy.

He might be in the winners' enclosure but Iain Duffus's face is a mask of pain at losing out yet again to teammate David Jefferies in 1999 as V&M team boss Jack Valentine looks on.

Joy

As Joey Dunlop mounted his SP 1 Honda in the winners' enclosure after the 2000 Formula One TT some wit asked if the 'oul fella' would be able to get his leg over it. 'Oul fella, och aye!' Joey retorted, in a jovial, split-second reaction. It was alright for him to joke about being too old and having to take it easy, but he had just won the best TT race of his career at 48 and he was taking no stick from anyone else!

LEFT: Phillip McCallen is barely able to lift the huge 'Winged Eros' trophy after his exertions during the 1997 Senior TT. Having avoided disaster in a crash at Quarry Bends in the Lightweight race on Monday, McCallen finished TT race week in 1997 by winning the Senior on Friday. The line between success and failure is that thin.

FAR LEFT: I have never seen a motorcycle racer who enjoyed racing more than Owen McNally, and he could not hide his ecstasy after finishing runner-up to Ian Lougher in the Ultra-Lightweight (125cc) TT in June 1999. McNally was killed the following August at the Ulster Grand Prix.

Against all odds

Dean Cooper

On a grey mizzly afternoon on 4 July 2000 I was running up a road on the Mid Antrim 150 course trying to find a decent vantage point to photograph the 600cc race that was just about to begin. Before I'd found my spot the bikes were on the track and I stepped into a farm lane to shoot the warm-up lap. When the riders had passed I just had time to get round the next corner to where I wanted to go. A few minutes later, on the opening lap of the race, Dean Cooper crashed his 600cc Kawasaki at the exact spot where I had been standing in the lane.

Fate had dealt a hand in my favour, but for Dean Cooper, who was to lose the lower part of his leg as a result of his injuries, the crash was the beginning of a new race.

Dean Cooper, No. 88, rounds the bend on the warm-up lap of the 600cc race at the 2000 Mid-Antrim 150. The crash happened a few minutes later, on the first racing lap.

LEFT: Medics attend to Dean Cooper's injuries at the scene. He remained conscious throughout the ordeal, and the horrific injury to his left foot can be clearly seen in this picture taken a few seconds after the crash.

Getting his false knee down at Tournagrough bend during the 2003 Dundrod 150. Dean was to set his fastest ever lap of the Dundrod course after the loss of his lower left leg.

BELOW: A clip on his left boot attaches the prosthesis to the footrest of the race bike, preventing it from slipping off but allowing the artificial limb to come away from the bike in the event of an accident.

Dean takes up the story:

'I hit the hedge at about 100mph, the bike went through it into the field and I bounced along the top before I ended up on the road. When all the smashing about was over I was still conscious and I was just lying there thinking that this is a pain in the arse because I was going to be out of action for a few races. There was a stinging sensation in my left foot, but I'd broken a few bones in crashes in the ten years or so that I'd been racing and I just thought it was another broken ankle. On the road to the hospital I knew by the way people were talking around me in the ambulance that maybe it was wee bit more serious this time. But it was still a big shock when the hospital doctor told me straight away that part of the leg would have to come off.

'After I was told I remember calling my father over and telling him to make sure he stayed around because if I fell asleep these people were going to cut off my

leg. I just couldn't take it in. The technical term for the injury was that my foot had been "degloved". Maybe it was barbed wire or a thorn stick in the hedge that I crashed into, but whatever it was it caught the skin and ripped it right off my foot leaving the bone and tissue raw right up to my ankle. In other words, my foot had been skinned. The doctors decided not to amputate it straight away, they gave me time to get used to the idea of losing it, and to tell you the truth by the end of the week I was begging them to cut it off. My foot became severely gangrenous and it was so stinking it made me want to throw up all the time. On top of that I had a collapsed lung, a broken collarbone, a dislocated shoulder, a shattered arm and busted ribs, so I was really uncomfortable and all my body's defences were becoming exhausted trying to fight the infection in my foot. Blood poisoning set in and I could feel myself draining away, so by the time the doctors said they would amputate I couldn't get the consent form signed soon enough.

'As soon as the operation was over I started to feel better and I wanted a goal, something to work towards. I just seemed to come to terms with the amputation immediately and I started to think and talk about racing again. The day I got out of the hospital I phoned the race doctor who'd told me that if I wanted to have another go he would organise the tests and so on. Over the next few months I had a special leg made for racing and a boot with a clip on the sole to keep it on the footrest. We modified the race bike with a right-foot gear change and a left-hand thumb-brake that took a bit of time to get used to. There was a whole rigmarole of safety tests and procedures to go through but I passed them all and was declared fit to race again.

Doctors helped design a special artificial limb to allow Dean Cooper to race again following his crash.

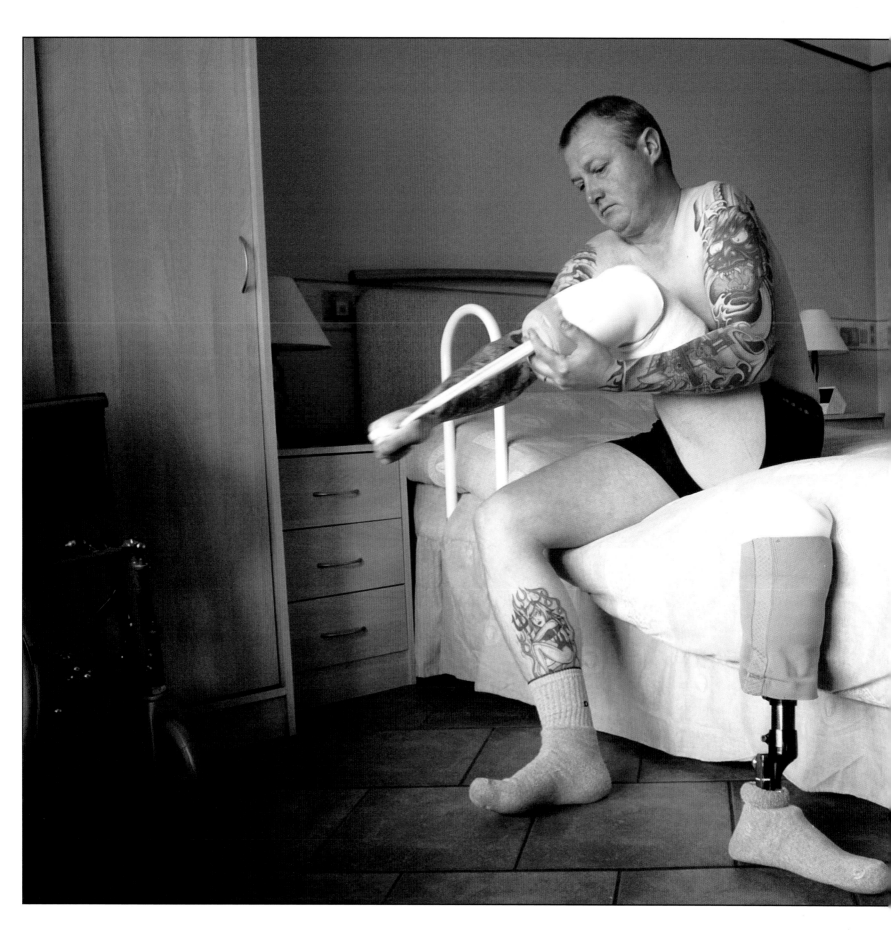

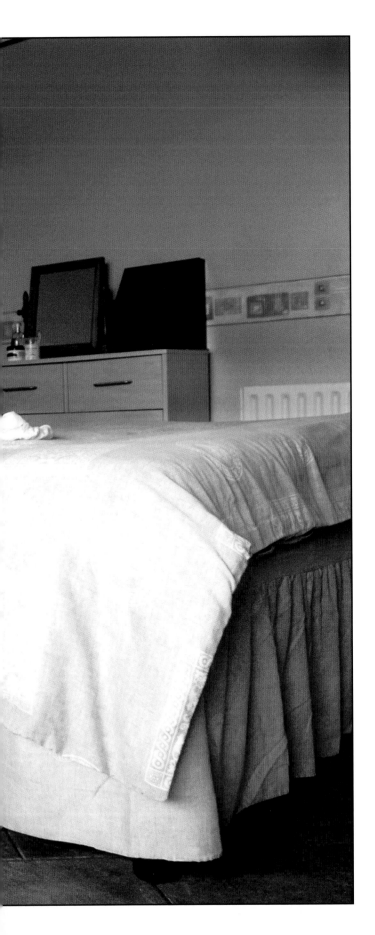

'I'd talked the whole racing thing over with my father and we'd agreed that it would be great if I could go out and just beat one other person and finish the race. I wouldn't be humiliating myself, which was my greatest fear. But it didn't work that way at all.

'As soon as I got on the bike I saw myself as exactly the same as everyone else – I didn't feel disabled at all. My biggest physical problem wasn't the leg but the arm that I'd broken. The surgeons had inserted a 14-inch steel pin into it and there was very little movement. That was my real hindrance.

'I did a series of track races to get my race licence for the roads again and by the start of 2003 I was going as fast as I ever had. In the practice for the Cookstown 100 I was third fastest in the 600cc class, with only Farquhar and Britton ahead of me and Archibald, Lindsay and the rest of the top boys behind me. Of course the officials wouldn't let me race in the main race as I had been put back into the Support class because of my leg, but I won two races on the day. It was great to be back racing, but the best bit was that I was competitive. I had good runs at Tandragee and the Dundrod 150 before I went back to the Mid Antrim, where I'd crashed in 2000. I didn't back off one inch on the corner it happened at and I remember smiling inside the helmet and thinking "I've beat you". It was a really good feeling.

'I've stopped racing now but I might come back, I'm not sure. I did take a couple of little tosses off the bike, and a lady in the crowd fainted at Athea when I crashed in front of her and my leg came off! The marshal was so relieved when he ran over to pick me up and I told him it was OK, that it was a false leg that was still attached to the bike! I can laugh at it because, to tell you the truth, I've never been happier in my life than I am now. Maybe it's because I feel I've been given a second chance, but I don't feel any bitterness at all about what has happened. Some people say road racing is mad, and yes, it is a kind of madness in a way, this need to race burning away inside you. It's definitely selfish and I think a lot about that when I remember my wife sitting crying beside the hospital bed. Racing has cost me dearly, but in spite of all that has happened, I love the sport and I hate to hear people attack it. It has given me a massive amount of enjoyment and if the clock was turned back I'd love to do it all again.'

The daily ritual of attaching his artificial leg is a constant reminder for Dean Cooper of the high price he has paid to be a road racer. But he has come to terms with this permanent disability. 'I can put it on in thirty seconds,' he says, 'and I don't let it stop me doing anything I want to do.'

The Chicken Catcher

Kenny McCrea

Working in the stifling, dusty heat of a huge broiler house, Kenny McCrea can catch ten thousand chickens on a good day, and every morning and evening he milks fifty-four cows on the family farm at Tynan in County Armagh. Except on weekends, when he forgets all about the day jobs and dons his bright blue-and-yellow leathers to race his 600cc Yamaha around Irish road courses such as Kells and Killalane.

Holding down two jobs hasn't stopped Kenny running up a bill of over £100,000 for his racing in the past ten years. 'A few years back I bought two bikes for the season. It cost me £21,000 by the time I'd bought them and set them up for racing,' he explains. 'It nearly put my lights out – and I'm still paying for it!' At the start of every year Kenny buys a bike on hire purchase, pays it off over the summer months and sells it in the autumn to repay the rest of the loan. 'It all works out fine as long as I don't crash and twist it. So far I've been lucky.'

This level of dedication and commitment might be understandable if it was earning the thirty-year-old a living, but that is far from the case. Kenny has never won a race in his life.

'I'd be lucky if I've won a thousand quid over the years,' he laughs. 'But it's worth every penny. Every single penny.' As is so often the case, there were always bikes in the McCrea family, and as soon as Kenny saw his first race, the Cookstown 100 in 1987, when he was twelve years old, he knew he would race some day. 'It just stayed in my mind,' he remembers.

Kenny McCrea at work in one of his two day jobs, catching chickens in a County Armagh broiler house in 2005.

Milking cows on the family dairy farm in Tynan, County Armagh. Kenny needs both jobs to provide the funds to race.

Much has been sacrificed to pursue the dream. For most people being a farmer is a full-time job, but Kenny's involvement in racing has distracted him from the family vocation. 'If I'd thrown myself into the farm I could have built it up into a good living by now. My parents get frustrated that I won't go that way but I'm into the bikes now and I just can't get out,' he explains.

Time and time again when you talk to road racers they describe their racing as a drug, something outside of themselves that has a hold on them that they just can't break, and for Kenny there is still unfinished business in racing. His ambition is to win the Manx Grand Prix before he quits. He lost a good friend in the 2004 race and finished fourth himself, but there is still a burning desire to compete and achieve something that farming can never offer. Other things have to stay on hold as well. 'My girlfriend Lesley is talking about us getting married but it's out of the question for now,' Kenny explains. Lesley's attitude to Kenny's racing is pragmatic – 'If you're happy, I'm happy' – but her apprehension is obvious on race days. 'I don't go well when she's there,' he says.

In a curious paradox the escape has become the problem, but the County Armagh farmer spends little time analysing this. When he does have a crash the first thing he wonders about is whether he will still be fit to do the milking. But life is there to be lived, not planned, and racing offers more excitement than anything else. 'When you are flying through Kerrowmoar and Glentramman, holding it flat open, there's nothing like it,' he grins.

LEFT: Unable to conceal her concern, Kenny McCrea's girlfriend Lesley bites her nails as she sits in the van in the Cookstown paddock and listens to his progress on the race commentary.

Last-minute checks as Kenny prepares to race at the 2005 Cookstown 100.

BELOW: Kenny gets a good-luck kiss from Lesley before heading off to the grid for the start of the Cookstown 100 in 2005.

The Mussel Man

John McGuinness

We weren't on the beach two minutes and he was in the water, scraping the mussels into the sieve and shaking them through it to gather the bigger ones that he could sell. Not the sort of work you might expect to find an eight-times Isle of Man TT winner engaged in, but its familiar graft to John McGuinness. As a 'Morecambe lad, born and bred' he is in his element on the huge strand. 'I bought my first proper race bike, a 1992 TZ 250 Yamaha, from the money I made out of collecting mussels,' John remembers proudly; an honest return for an honest day's work. 'I love coming out here,' he says looking round at the vast expanse of Morecambe Bay.

Born in the Cumbrian town in 1972, McGuinness was drawn to the sea and a trade as a bricklayer until his talent on two wheels emerged. He served his racing time on the English short circuits, cadging tyre warmers from Steve Hislop and rummaging through the Dunlop used-tyre bin for race rubber when he started circuit racing in the early 1990s. But it was the roads, and the TT in particular, that had captured his imagination from an early age. 'I first went to the Isle of Man in 1987 on my BMX; we stopped in a tent and I saw Hizzy win,' he laughs. Even as a youngster, McGuinness was sure of his destiny. 'I was in Joey Dunlop's garage in 1988. I had seen him up on the winners' rostrum the day before and I told him that someday I would be standing up there beside him.'

John McGuinness collects mussels on Morecambe Bay in May 2005. McGuinness launched his racing career on the bike he bought with the proceeds of mussel and cockle picking.

In 1999 he achieved that ambition, finishing third in the Lightweight (250cc) TT behind Dunlop and Ian Lougher, and John reminded the Ballymoney man of his youthful prediction as they sprayed the champagne together. In the early years the Morecambe man's TT career parallelled that of his good friend David Jefferies. 'We made our debuts in 1996,' John recalls. Both men had tasted major TT success before the horrendous accident that claimed the Yorkshireman's life in 2003. McGuinness was just a few seconds behind his best friend and rode into the debris of the crash.

'Seeing David lying there was the very worst thing I've experienced in racing. It was hard to go on after that. It was all just a blur and I didn't want to race, but there's just something that drives you on. Or maybe it's just that there isn't something that stops you.'

McGuinness on the receiving end of a champagne shower from Adrian Archibald and Bruce Anstey on the Formula One TT podium in 2004.

Getting through that experience, and going on to impose the same kind of authority that DJ enjoyed during his last few years in the toughest motorcyle sporting event in the world, requires a strength of mind that few possess.

'It's not being disrespectful, but you can't let thoughts of the dangers and the crashes get lodged in your mind. To go on you mustn't look, you have to turn away, that's how you survive. I'm not religious at all but every time I race the TT I say a prayer to the riders who have gone. I feel they are looking down and I ask them to look after me.'

Few road racers will ever be this candid about their deepest thoughts. Very, very few riders will ever watch a race themselves – it's just too close to the danger. Most will simply tell you that they don't think about the risks at all, they won't even go there in their own heads. To do so would be to admit a weakness that a more strong-minded opponent might exploit. But John McGuinness is a man who has weighed up the dangers and the options he has in the sport, and he has made his choice.

FAR LEFT: Exiting the Gooseneck, John McGuinness powers his R1 Yamaha up onto the mountain during practice for the 2004 TT.

'I've done lots of things on bikes besides the road racing and I've ridden with the best in the world. I've raced in the British Grand Prix against the likes of Doohan and Rossi. Over the last few years there has been the British Superbike championship for me, and in 1999 I was 250cc British champion on the circuits. We lived for years with Becky's parents and I poured every single penny I earned into racing. I've been reached nothing, but bikes have been my life and if it has cost me everything I don't feel I have sacrificed anything because that's what I wanted.'

Over the last couple of seasons the former mussel and cockle picker has made a bit of money with his TT success, so he continues racing the most dangerous course in the world and shrouding the risks in black humour. 'If I get squashed you'll have to do it yourself,' he says to Becky with a laugh as he refuses to do a chore he doesn't fancy. It is just another way of dealing with the fear. If it can't be met with out-and-out denial then it has to be laughed at. 'I'm not bothered' is a stock McGuinness response.

With the constant risk of injury and a tenuous reliance on brittle machinery, it would be a foolish road racer who looked to money for his prime motivation; the prize funds are meagre when set against the risks. John McGuinness is no fool.

RIGHT: One famous Morecambe son alongside another: John McGuinness mimics the statue of comedian Eric Morecambe that stands on the town's promenade.

The McGuinness garage is full of memorabilia from his racing career.

Hammering the Triumph Daytona into Memorial Bends, John McGuinness gives the British bike its final race outing on home soil at the Scarborough Gold Cup in September 2004.

LEFT: **His face a mask of concentration, John McGuinness wheelies the AIM R1 Yamaha over Ago's Leap at 180mph on his way to winning the inaugural Superbike TT in 2005.**

The joy of winning and the relief at having survived the dangers of racing at incredible speed on the TT course are etched on John McGuinness's face as he hugs his son Ewan in the winners' enclosure after the Superbike race in 2005.

No racer is more steeped in the history of the sport, and he talks with obvious pride and pleasure about his own racing achievements in comparison to the figures of old. But it is something much deeper that pulls him in. 'Seeing my son Ewan's face in the winners' enclosure after I won the Formula One TT in 2004 was the best thing of all, he was just so proud of his Dad. Not making that happen, not being successful, that's the greatest fear.'

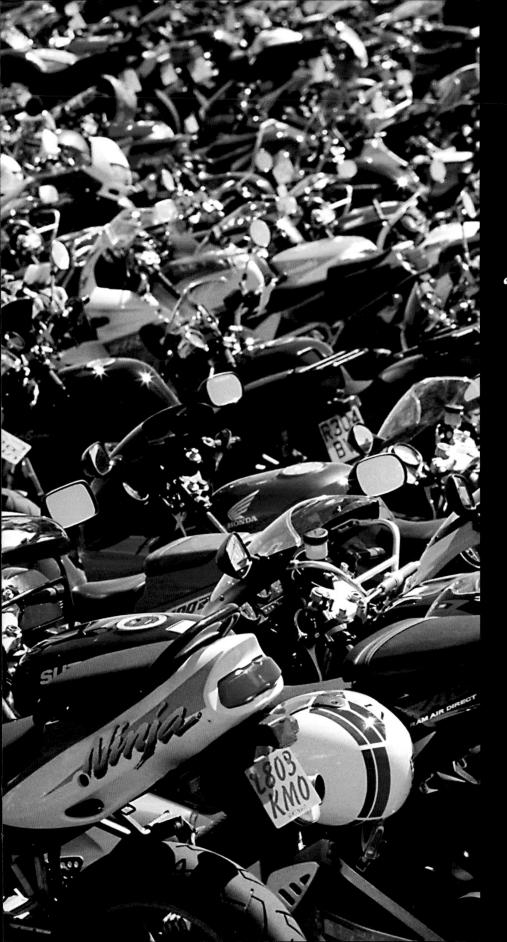

The Obsessed
Road racing fans

'**D**'you see your man over there?' said my informant, pointing. 'Well he's got the best racing tattoo you've ever seen in your life — Joey Dunlop's all over his back.' A few moments later 'your man' was pulling his shirt over his head, displaying his indelible mark of devotion to road racing for my camera. It was indeed a fine piece of work, lovingly executed by his brother, a tattoo artist by trade, over many hours of excruciating pain. Although this particular display of affection for the sport was slightly more extreme than the norm, there is no shortage of devoted followers in motorcycle road racing.

Stand beside a couple of old-timers on any Irish road race ditch and you will soon hear them recounting how many years they have been attending the 'Nor' West' or the 'Prix'; anything under thirty years is hardly worth mentioning and, of course, the 'service' has to be 'unbroken'.

It's not like going to a football or rugby match. You don't buy your ticket at the gate and get a seat with a number on it for an hour and a half. Roads close early and open late and you're there for the duration. Creature comforts are still few and far between – a toilet, other than a discreet spot behind a hedge, is still a rarity – and a good seat consists of dry grass with no thorns. Whilst there is plenty of camaraderie in bike racing you can't really feel part of a 'Kop' or 'Stretford End' when you're perched on the edge of a mountain road with no other living company than a couple of passing crows.

Road racing is more of an individual experience, and what you lose out on in modern luxury you gain in sensory joy. It may be a mile from the nearest burger van and the hole in the hedge might only be big enough for a ten-year-old, but there is something childlike in the adventure of taking your sandwiches and flask and crawling in to feel the excited apprehension as you lie in wait for the bikes. There's time to think, to realise that you are never this close to nature, so close that the grass is tickling your nose, the insects are crawling up your sleeves. Then you hear them coming, the distant roar of screaming engines, piling on the pressure, terrifying the birds off the branches. You're tensed now in an almost unbearable wait, wanting to see them, to be thrilled and scared and in awe all at once. They are a hundred yards away when they break into sight, but they cover that distance in a split-second blur of colour and outrageous speed, and then it's over, for another lap at least. To witness such speed this close up, so close you could reach out and touch it if you were foolish enough, is an immense pleasure – and strangely, at times, a huge relief. In 2004, I was at Budore bend taking photographs of the Superbike race at the Ulster Grand Prix. A five-way battle between Bruce Anstey, John McGuinness, Ian Lougher, Ryan Farquhar and Adrian Archibald was bringing almost 1000bhp snaking up the hill towards me, their thunderous roar captured under the trees of Quarterland's and Ireland's and booming up the green tunnel. I was lying at the edge of the road full of fear, so scared that the lens was shaking in my hands as the five of them blasted round the 170mph bend as one, scraping the tarmac with their knees, dust and sparks flying. Their departure left the air full of the stench of burning rubber from hot, tortured tyres, and my heart full of a delicious relief. That intense build-up, the growing dread and terror of what might happen if one of them got it wrong or a tyre burst or an engine seized, or, or, or … all of that was over and they were gone and I could breathe again. You feel that huge sense of relief, yet you're left wondering – if it's like that for me, what the hell is it like for them?

Where else could you get this close to 170mph?
Fans line the fences and ditches at Paddock Bend during
the 2004 Athea road races in County Limerick.

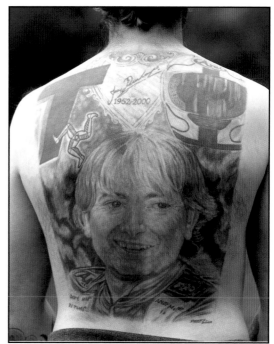

ABOVE LEFT:
A familiar face and smile at every Irish road race – Mick the Marshal.

ABOVE RIGHT:
The ultimate tribute to the ultimate road racer? A fan pays homage to Joey Dunlop.

RIGHT:
Spectators introduce a few home comforts to the undergrowth with a vodka optic at Ireland's Bend, Dundrod.

The challenge for this TT fan was to drink the pint of beer in his right hand before the flames creeping up the toilet paper reached his backside. No chance!

115

LEFT: Seeking the ultimate 'Kodak moment' at Skerries in 2004.

Been there, done it, got the badge!

BELOW: Every hole in every hedge is a grandstand seat at a road race.

Armco Alley
Macau Grand Prix

As soon as you step off the jetfoil from Hong Kong and smell the aroma of fried noodles blasting from every air conditioning unit in the endless blocks of tenements of this Chinese city, you know that the Macau Grand Prix will be a very different road race from Monaghan or the Mid Antrim. A former Portuguese colony, Macau is the Monte Carlo of the East, home to a glittering array of sumptuous hotels and inviting casinos as well as the venue for a surreal festival of car and bike racing through streets normally clogged with the densest traffic in the world.

Sharing its Special Administrative Region status with Hong Kong, Macau has armed soldiers of the Red Army on silent and statue-like duty at the Chinese government headquarters in the city.

There are brolly-dollies galore in Macau!

Armco barriers trail back into the distance as Martin Finnegan leads a line of riders up Moorish Hill during practice for the 2003 Macau Grand Prix.

Michael Rutter cranks the Red Bull Honda Fireblade into Solitude Bends with the city's office blocks in the background. The catch fencing was put on top of the wall a few years ago after a car mounted the wall and careered over the cliff behind it.

LEFT: Michael Rutter makes final preparations in his garage before the start of the 2004 Macau Grand Prix. Rutter's superbly smooth style is well suited to the Guia circuit and he has become the recent dominant force in the Chinese race, winning five times since 1998.

But there seem to be few excesses of western-style life that the Communist regime will not turn a blind eye to, and Macau revels in an exciting subversity. Encountering such a culture shock apparently requires major acclimatisation for the bike racing contingent, and the organisers ship the riders and their machines to Macau several days before practice begins each November. It is a moot point whether early-hours sessions in the Irish bar (yes, even Macau has one, run by a man from Cookstown, County Tyrone) is what the well-meaning race directors have in mind by acclimatisation! But it's all part of the holiday race atmosphere that pervades the event for the bike racers. With the Formula Three cars hogging the limelight on the 3.8-mile Guia circuit (as it is known locally), the two-wheeled contingent are reduced to a sideshow, amounting to just a couple of brief qualifying sessions and a half-hour race. For the riders, crouched on a race bike and suffering in the searing heat and humidity, that is probably long enough, but the South China Sea is an awfully long way to go for a couple of hours' worth of action photographs.

Half a million people are crammed into the nine square kilometres that comprise the Macau Peninsula, and most of them live in huge tenement blocks.

Perhaps the best thing about capturing this image in 2003 was Steve Plater's reaction when I showed it to him in the pits a few minutes later. He stared at it for a few moments in silence, then whooped in jubilation and ran off with my digital camera to show his mechanics! It had been an incredible moment as he plunged into the Solitude Esses just a little too hot and brushed his right shoulder along the yellow wall on the exit. You are never sure if you've caught the picture: if you see it through the camera it usually means you've missed it. Down the years I had heard all the stories about Steve Hislop hitting his helmet on the wall at Barregarrow and Phillip McCallen brushing his leathers off bales tied to telegraph poles at the Isle of Man TT, but I had never seen any photographs of it happening. I couldn't really believe that this was what it looked like, and neither could Steve. He had been fighting the 600cc Honda all the way around the corner in the bright morning sunshine, and with the throttle closing I could actually hear the hiss of his leathers against the yellow concrete. After I showed him the picture Steve showed me the yellow paint on his shoulder; we both had our trophies from the day.

Germany's Markus Barth rides the line up San Francisco Hill on his R1 Yamaha in 2003, trying to ignore the line of covered parking meters just over the Armco barrier.

What action it is though. The dangers of the street circuit literally stare you in the face as workers toil day and night to erect miles of catch fencing and metal barriers. Macau is the only bike-racing track in the world with zero run-off. In Ireland and the Isle of Man there is the occasional soft hedge to break a rider's fall if he goes down, but on these city streets there are only Armco barriers and concrete walls. If that were not enough of a disincentive to crashing, anyone who does get it wrong won't be asked back to this invitation-only event.

The bikes scream off the line down a wide four-lane boulevard between glitzy skyscrapers into Lisboa, the corner named after the hotel casino that is Macau's most famous landmark. From here the circuit changes dramatically as it leaves the slippery taxi rank in front of the hotel marking the end of the seafront section to climb San Francisco Hill, past the hospital and up on to the winding cliff-top road. The track is much narrower here, and the riders brush their shoulders against the walls before plunging down Moorish Hill and around Donna Maria Bend into the impossibly tight Melcoo hairpin. Built, like so much of Macau, on land reclaimed from the sea, the final section of the course is flat and superfast. To see the bikes hammering down the last mile past noodle shops and tiny workshops into the busy city centre is one of the most awesome sights in road racing. But strangely, it is an attraction that seems to pass the locals by.

O'Kane Suzuki teammates Richard Britton (No. 18) and Stephen Thompson follow each other during early-morning Macau practice in 2004 as the sun lights up the city backdrop.

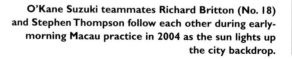

ABOVE: On every lap of final practice local rider IP Weng Keong came down to this corner, put his shoulder against the wall and rode round it like this. At over 80mph! But he failed to win any home advantage from his antics because he finished the race in 33rd position on his R6 Yamaha – dead last!

RIGHT: Jose Leite's eyes are full of the total concentration required to steer his ZX 10 Kawasaki between the Macau hazards.

BELOW RIGHT: One slip and this is how it can all end up in Macau. Austrian Erwin Wilding slammed into the Armco barrier on the blindingly fast first corner during practice in 2004. The front forks were ripped off the Honda Fireblade before it burst into flames. Fortunately, Wilding lived to tell the tale.

Apart from those in the official grandstands, spectators are actively discouraged from watching the racing by gun-toting policemen who check every pass and make it clear that their word is final.

Dozens of the world's top racers have ridden these streets since Japanese rider Hiroshi Hasegawa won the first bike Grand Prix in Macau in 1967. His countryman Sadeo Asami won a hat-trick of races between 1978 and 1980, before 'Rocket' Ron Haslam stamped his authority on the event in 1981, going on to win six times, an all-time record. Michael Rutter is now creeping up on that total, with five wins since 1998. Other well-known British road racers who have won in Macau include Mick Grant, Robert Dunlop, Steve Hislop, Carl Fogarty, Phillip McCallen, David Jefferies and John McGuinness, but perhaps the most illustrious of all Macau winners was Texan Kevin Schwantz in 1988. The Grand Prix world champion had never set eyes on Macau before, but he won what was then a two-leg race, even though he spent most of the time wheelieing around the course.

It was no surprise, really, as he had been over seven seconds faster than his closest rival, Jamie Whitham, in practice.

Playing checkers in the park

A friendly encounter with the Macanese

Schwantz came to Macau as one of the best motorcyle racers in the world, but drivers from the four-wheel brigade often visit Macau on the way to the top of their sport. Victory on the Guia circuit was one of the stepping stones on the way to Formula One greatness for both Ayrton Senna and Michael Schumacher.

Whilst cars do have a parallel event in Monaco, Macau is like no other road race for motorcycles.

Apart from being incredibly dangerous and stupendously fast, the most extraordinary thing is the noise. It is spine-tingling to hear the shriek of the engines caught between the massive buildings as they hurtle at full throttle down the city streets, and you just can't quite believe how fast they are going given the number of things there are to hit if there is a crash.

2002 Macau Grand Prix winner John McGuinness glides his elbow along the Armco barrier on the Monstermob Ducati in 2004. Inch perfect, he was only a foot away from my lens.

2003 Macau winner Michael Rutter helps runner-up
John McGuinness cool down by pouring water down
the neck of his leathers on the podium.

In 2004 Michael Rutter was sliding his bright blue Honda
Fireblade sideways into Lisboa on every lap, riding right up to
the Armco on the exit. One slip and it would have been
disaster. Most of the racers will tell you that it is the most
perilous place they race, but they all want to come back year
after year and it's easy to see why. Apart from the challenge
of the circuit, Macau's contrasts have a hypnotic appeal. The
teeming city streets are filled with every form of life: priests
rub shoulders with prostitutes and the fabulously wealthy
step around limbless beggars. The run-down colonial
architecture of the old city and its warren of filthy streets
give way to massive, modern hotels and casinos that echo
Las Vegas. The tranquil, secluded beauty of Buddhist temples
offers an oasis of quiet after the overcrowded streets where
two people stopping to pass the time of day on the pavement
instantly causes a huge logjam of frustrated humanity. It is an
extraordinary race venue, but you would never dream of
going to Macau just for the racing.

The ecstatic team of Portuguese rider Rui Reigoto celebrate
his finishing the 2004 Macau Grand Prix. The Suzuki rider
clinched 16th place, but it is the triumph over adversity that
gives the greatest pleasure in completing this race.

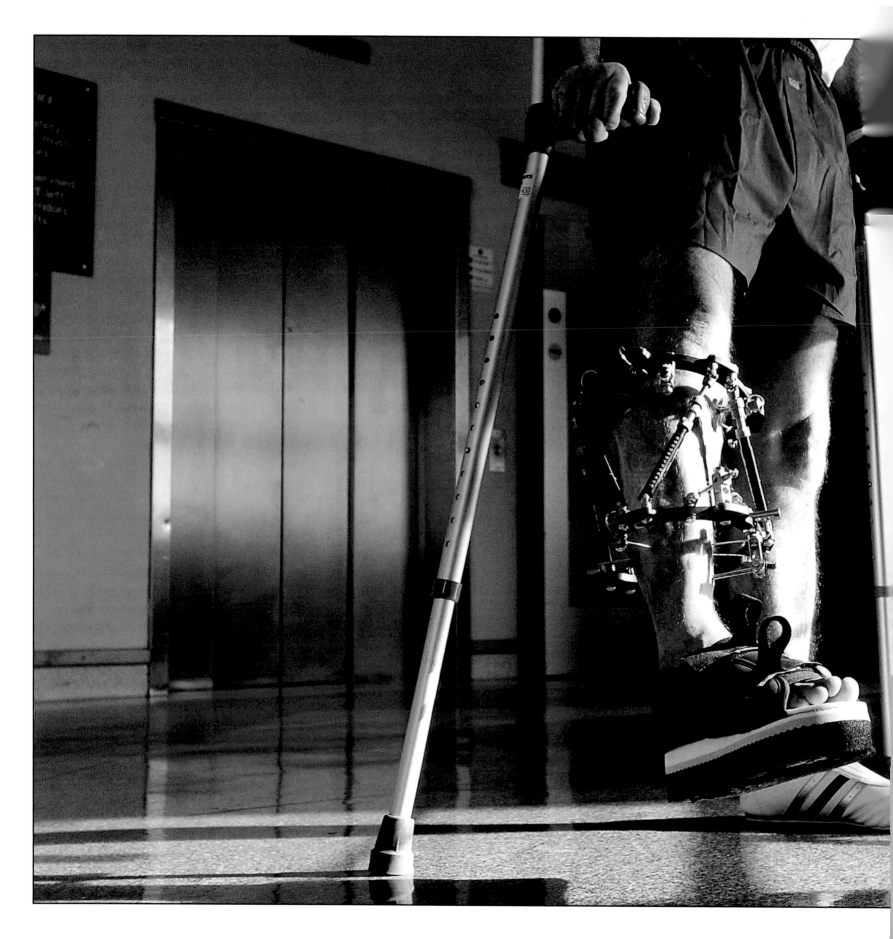

Hard as Nails

Robert Dunlop

When the back wheel of Robert Dunlop's RC45 Honda disintegrated at over 100mph as he blasted through Ballaugh village in the 1994 Isle of Man TT, the tiny racer was fired straight into a stone wall. Most observers felt that the horrendous injuries he received to his right arm and leg would see him fired into racing history. But the Ballymoney man didn't share their pessimism – if he could walk he could ride, and if he could ride he could race. It took time and some machine modifications – as well as some huge arguments with race officials – for Dunlop to overcome the hindrances of nerve damage to his right hand and restricted movement in his right leg, but his determination to get back to winning never wavered. In 1998 he returned to the TT to beat the course that had hurt him so badly four years earlier, winning the Ultra-Lightweight (125cc) TT.

Before the 1994 crash Robert Dunlop was one of the best riders in the world. He had won the British championship on the English short circuits, triumphed at the TT and become the most successful rider ever at the North West 200. As a works rider with Norton he had seemed almost invincible on the roads, but all of that changed when he hammered into that Ballaugh wall. No longer able to physically control a big bike, Robert was restricted to the smaller 125cc machines. The horizons may have narrowed but Dunlop's ambitions did not, and he went on to become a master of the 'tiddler' class and win countless races on the little screamers.

Robert Dunlop leaves Musgrave Park hospital, Belfast, after an operation to lengthen and straighten his damaged right leg in February 2005. The surgeons attached the cage directly to the bone with steel wire and Robert adjusted it himself over several months, stretching the bone a few millimetres every day.

The most successful North West 200 rider in history, with fourteen victories, Robert Dunlop wheelies the JPS Norton to another win in 1990.

Only in 2004, ten years after the crash, and having achieved all that he wanted to achieve on a racing motorbike, did Robert Dunlop turn his attention to dealing with the damage to his right leg, which is two inches shorter than the left leg and a couple of inches out of line. He has had an adjustable cage fitted to the leg to stretch and straighten it. Every day he adjusts the screws himself, one millimeter at a time, stretching the bone in his own leg with his own hands. He has had over a dozen operations on this leg alone.

Pain is no barrier for the top road racers. It is accepted as part of the deal, and only the inconvenience of the injury is a problem.

After his 1994 TT crash, Robert was unable to control the larger-capacity machines with his mangled limbs, forcing him to concentrate his efforts on the 125cc machines. On his way to winning at the final Carrowdore 100 race on the Crossan Honda in 2000, he 'rests' his arm as he passes the petrol station in the County Down village.

A Dunlop family day out. Robert, sons Michael (wearing white T-shirt) and William and nephew Sam (wearing cap) spectate between races at Athea in 2004.

Head to head, Robert and his son William form a continuous line of road racing heritage as they work on Robert's bike in the Athea paddock in 2004.

LEFT: In the master's footsteps. William Dunlop follows his father as they race their 125cc machines at Kells in 2004.

BELOW: Undeterred by the cumbersome leg brace or the freezing cold wind, Robert Dunlop is engrossed in fixing the brakes on his son Michael's bike at Bishopscourt short circuit in County Down in March 2005.

Mischievous and full of fun in spite of his injury problems,
Robert produced this 'paddock bike' and proceeded to lap the
backyard on it during this visit to his Ballymoney home.

Road racers judge injuries not by how much they are suffering but by how much their performance on the bike is affected. I have heard them discuss the loss of a finger not in degrees of pain but in terms of whether losing it from the clutch hand or throttle hand was the most inconvenient for machine control. When he won that famous TT race in 1998, Robert Dunlop was actually riding with a broken leg protected by a special cast. He was receiving physiotherapy every single time he stepped off the bike. These men are as hard as nails.

Robert plays with his dogs, John and Finbar, at home in Ballymoney.

Although Robert has not ruled out a return to competition when the long healing process is completed, he now devotes most of his time to the racing efforts of his two sons, William and Michael. Surely the acid test for any road racer is whether or not he would allow his children to race. In spite of all that he has suffered himself, Robert Dunlop has clearly answered that question in the affirmative, and over the past few seasons Robert and William have had some great race battles, with the vast experience of the father in machine preparation and race craft being passed down the generations. The youngsters will have to learn to cope with the knocks the hard way though, by feeling the pain themselves. That is something that cannot be taught.

Robert Dunlop sitting by the stove in his Ballymoney home in 2005.

The knocks have never dimmed their father's zest for life. The impish grin and mischievous sense of humour still brighten the paddock. Even in injury and in pain Robert has never given up. He has been carried from hospital beds and set upon racing bikes. That strength of character is a family trait, and it is true that no family has gained so much from the sport. The Dunlop name is the most famous name in motorcycle road racing, though that honour has come at a terrible cost. Robert has lost a brother in the cruellest of ways, and the pain of his own personal suffering is obvious. Perhaps then there are times when all of the banter has died down, when the champagne has been spilled and the winner's garlands have withered, that Robert Dunlop sits alone and ponders these things. Was it worth it … ?

An unequal challenge? Robert Dunlop skims
the fearsome walls of Handley's Bend on his
tiny 125cc Honda during the 2003 TT.
With an incredible mountain of achievements
scaled over the last twenty-five years and the
bitter effects of the crash injuries now largely
overcome, he might be expected to hang up his
leathers. But with a man like Robert Dunlop,
who can ever be sure?

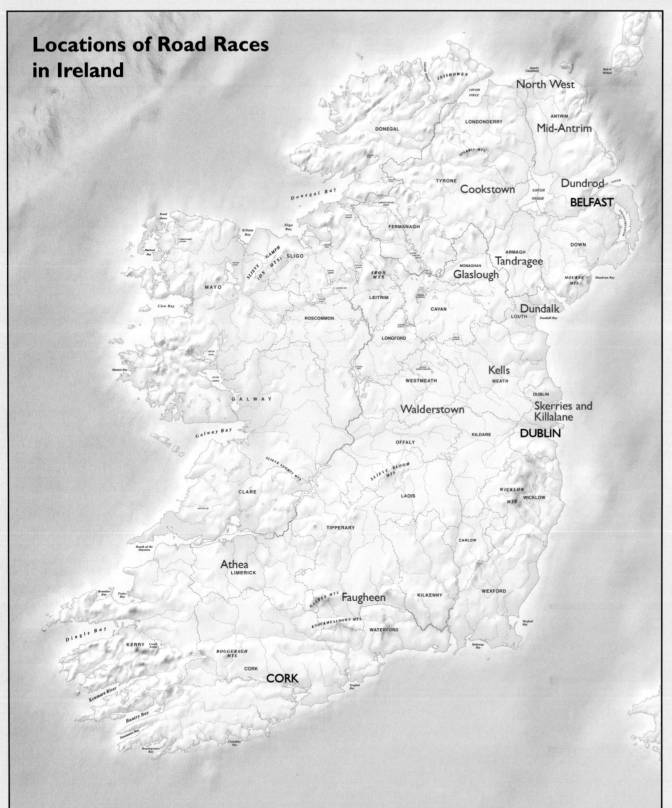

Locations of Road Races in Ireland

Thank you

to the women at Blackstaff Press, Belfast – Patsy Horton, who brought the idea of the book to life, Rachel McNicholl, who gave it direction, and Wendy Dunbar, who forged its shape

to my colleagues at Pacemaker Press International

and to all the road racers.

First published in October 2005 by Blackstaff Press
4c Heron Wharf
Sydenham Business Park
Belfast BT3 9LE, Northern Ireland

Reprinted November 2005

Text © Stephen Davison, 2005
Images by Stephen Davison © Pacemaker Press International, 2005
All rights reserved

Stephen Davison has asserted his right under the Copyright, Designs and Patents Act 1988 to be identified as the author of this work.

Printed in England by The Bath Press

A CIP catalogue record for this book is available from the British Library.

ISBN 0-85640-776-3

www.blackstaffpress.com
www.pacemakerpressintl.com